Who Says Hoo?

by Kevin J. Brougher & Lisa M. Santa Cruz

WHO SAYS HOO?

Missing Piece Press, LLC does not accept unsolicited manuscripts.
Visit: MissingPiecePress.com for information on our other fun products.
LIKE us on Facebook to keep up to date with our new books, games and special offers.
"A LITTLE Thinking...a LOT of fun!" is a trademark of Missing Piece Press, LLC.

*Missing Piece Press is a publisher
of award-winning books and games.
Our goal is to produce products that fill the user
with a sense of fun, wonder, and intrigue.*

Other Publications from Missing Piece Press

BOOKS

Thinklers! 1: *A Collection of Brain Ticklers!*

Thinklers! 2: *More Brain Ticklers!*

Thinklers! 3: *Even More Brain Ticklers!*

Thinklers! 4 : *Full-Color Brain Ticklers!*

History Mysteries: *A New Twist on Time-Lines*

State Debate: *50 Unique Playing Cards and 50 Games*

Number Wonders: *A Collection of Amazing Number Facts!*

Dreams, Screams, & JellyBeans!: *Poems for All Ages*

The Storybook: *A novel for ages 10 on up*

Science Stumpers: *Brain-Busting Scenarios...Solved with Science*

Algebra Summary Sheets: *Posters to Promote Proficiency*

Reindolphins: *A Christmas Tale*

Grandpa Kevin's ABC Book: *really kinda strange, somewhat bizarre and overly unrealistic*

GAMES

Frazzle: *A Frenzied Game of Words*

ShanJari: *An African Game of Sequence & Strategy*

Whew! : *Words, Wits, Whims & Woes!*

TooT! : *A Nerdy Little Game*

Blam! : *A Different Card Game*

DICE Blam! : *A Different Dice Game*

Word Nerd : *A Quick-Witted Word Game*

Bunco BUDDIES! : *The BETTER Bunco Game*

Besto : *An Animal Matching Game*

Crummy : *The Criss-Cross Rummy Game*

Take 12! : *The Token Taking Game*

Round About : *A Little Thinking a Lot of FUN!*

Crowns :*Got the CROWN? Control the round*

Rummage: *The Rummy Race Game!*

RUNZ: *The No-Sets-Allowed Game*

.....and more!

A Little Thinking...a LOT of FUN! ®

Missing Piece Press, LLC

For Alexander & Gabriel

Well, for Susie and Pamela, too. Really...it's for any young kid that likes animals. And...just to be clear, it can be for older kids - I am definitely **NOT** excluding older kids. You know...it can also be for **ADULTS**. I mean...hey, I am **NOT** saying adults can't enjoy this. In fact, I think they will. So, I guess, this book is for **EVERY** one out there. But, it's really, uh...mostly for Alexander and Gabriel. You know...I think it's time to just turn this page and get started.

Enjoy!

Meow, meow - says the cat,
as it stretches in the chair.
Meow, meow - says the cat,
with the fluffy gray hair.

meow
meow

cat

Woof, woof - says the dog,
as it goes to fetch some sticks.
Woof, woof - says the dog.
Now, watch for hugs and licks.

woof woof

dog

Moo, moo - says the cow,
in the grass so lush and green.
Moo, moo - he's the biggest -
the biggest cow I've seen!

moo
moo

COW

Neigh, Neigh - says the horse,
as he munches on some hay.
Neigh, neigh - now it's time -
time to run and play!

neigh
neigh

horse

Chirp, chirp - says the cricket,
in the warm air of the night.
Chirp, chirp - as he stares,
at the moon so big and bright.

chirp
chirp

cricket

Caw, caw - says the crow,
as he flies up over head.
Caw, caw - as he flies
to the nest he calls his bed.

caw
caw

crow

15

Oink, oink - says the pig -
in the mud he rolls around.
Oink, oink - is the pig's
funny grunting sound.

oink
oink

pig

Growl, growl - says the bear,
as it rubs against a tree.
Growl, growl - says the bear
as he's running from a bee.

growl
growl

bear

Buzz, buzz - says the bee,
as it starts to chase a bear.
Buzz, buzz - says the bee,
as it gets into its hair.

buzz
buzz

bee

Screech, screech - says the bat,
as it skims above the lake.
Screech, screech - as it flies
when most are not awake.

screech
screech

bat

Cluck, cluck - goes the chicken,
as it scratches on the ground.
Cluck, cluck - as it eats,
all the things it's found.

cluck
cluck

chicken

Click, click - says the dolphin,
as it splashes in the sea.
Click, click - says the dolphin,
so playful and so free.

click
click

dolphin

Quack, quack - says the duck.
as it waddles down the path.
Quack, quack - as it swims
in the lake to take a bath.

quack
quack

duck

Croak, croak - says the frog,
as he sits upon the log.
Croak, croak - then he leaps,
into the muddy bog.

croak
croak

frog

Who hoo - says the owl,
with eyes both big and round.
Who hoo - as it flies
with hardly any sound.

who
hoo

owl

Coo, coo - says the pigeon,
as it walks and bobs its head.
Coo, coo - as it finds
some freshly fallen bread.

coo coo

pigeon

Hiss, hiss - says the snake,
with his tongue he smells the air.
Hiss, hiss - as he slithers,
with no arms - no legs - no hair.

hiss
hiss

snake

Hee haw - says the donkey - he works most everyday.

Hee haw - says the donkey - it's also called a "BRAY".

hee hee haw

donkey

They all make lots of sounds through out the night and day.

I wonder what it is
that they are trying to say.

But, an elephant so big
or an ant so very small -
everyone should learn -
learn to LOVE them ALL!

The end.

For years of family enjoyment get our
award-winning Christmas Tale : Reindolphins

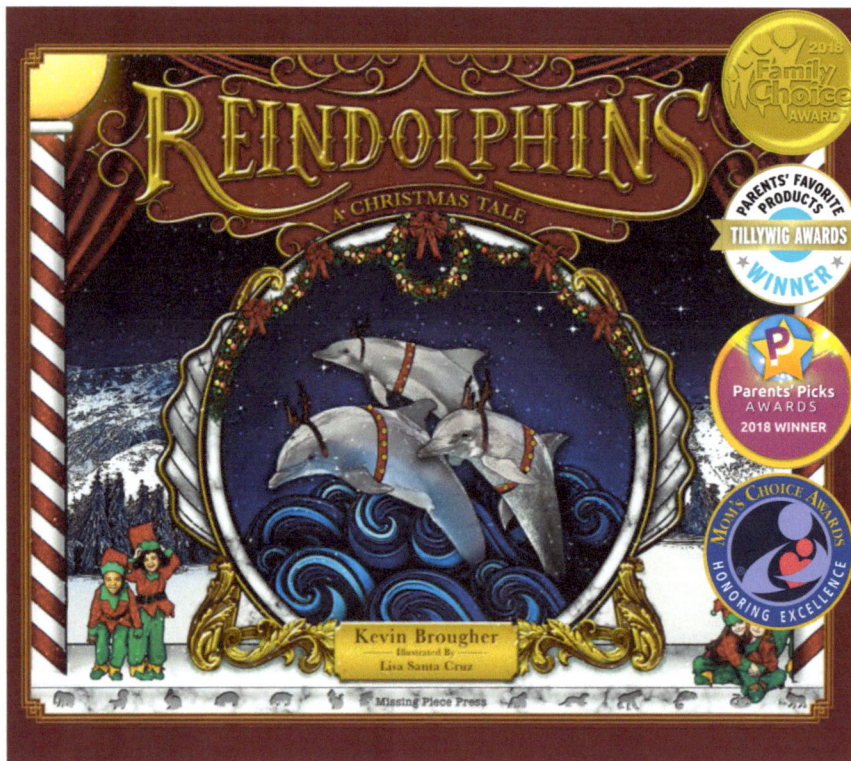

Lots of fun words for young and old.

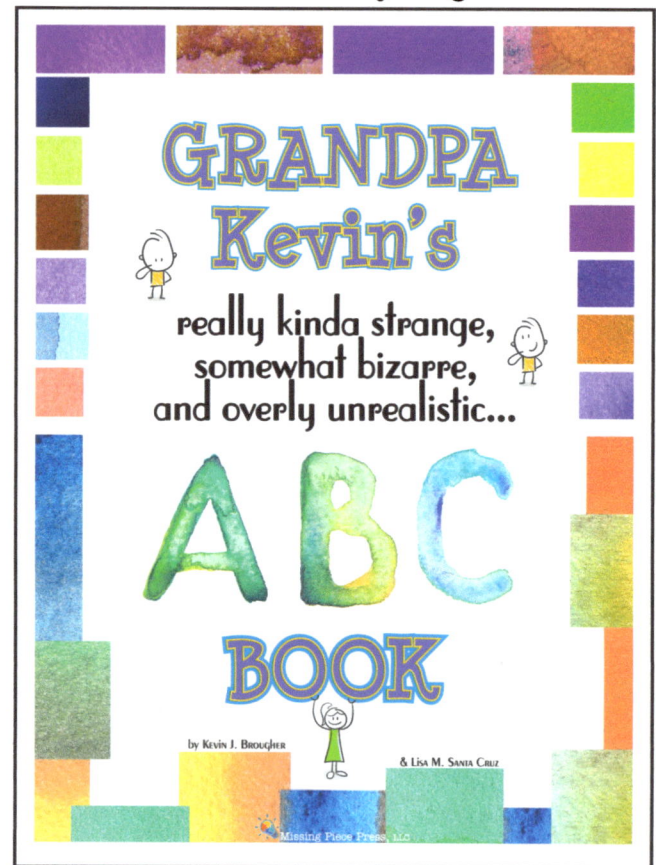

REINDOLPHINS
A CHRISTMAS TALE

2018 Family Choice AWARD

PARENTS' FAVORITE PRODUCTS
TILLYWIG AWARDS
WINNER

Parents' Picks AWARDS
2018 WINNER

MOM'S CHOICE AWARDS
HONORING EXCELLENCE

Kevin Brougher
Illustrated By
Lisa Santa Cruz

Missing Piece Press

GRANDPA Kevin's

really kinda strange,
somewhat bizarre,
and overly unrealistic...

ABC

BOOK

by Kevin J. Brougher

& Lisa M. Santa Cruz

Missing Piece Press, LLC

Missing Piece Press, LLC

www.ingramcontent.com/pod-product-compliance
Lightning Source LLC
Chambersburg PA
CBHW041552030426

42335CB00005B/191